Excel

BASIC SKILLS

ENGLISH

YEAR 3

AGES 8–9

ENGLISH WORKBOOK

Get the Results You Want!

PASCAL PRESS

Jane Baker

Reprinted 2006, 2007, 2009, 2010 (twice), 2011, 2013, 2016, 2018, 2020, 2022

ISBN 978 1 74125 156 2

Pascal Press
PO Box 250
Glebe NSW 2037
(02) 8585 4050
www.pascalpress.com.au

Publisher: Vivienne Joannou
Series developer: Kristine Brown
Project editor: Emma Driver
Edited by Christine Eslick
Page design and layout by Jelly Design
Typesetting by Replika Press
Cover by DiZign Pty Ltd
Photos by Comstock, Corel, Ingram Publishing, Photos.com and PhotoEssentials
Printed by Vivar Printing/Green Giant Press

Contents

Acknowledgements

The author and publisher would like to thank the following copyright holders for permission to reprint their Year 3 writings:

- Stephanie Compton
- Anthea Compton
- Kevin Baker
- Jack Sanderson

Grateful acknowledgement is made of the support of the teachers of the South Coast Region, NSW, and in particular of the assistance and encouragement given by Mrs Rhonda Bassett, Acting Principal, Bowning Public School.

To the student

When you work in this book you will be practising writing many of the texts you learn at school. Most of the sample texts (writing) in this book have been written by students in Year 3. Carefully read the sample text at the beginning of each chapter and check which special features of the writing are shown by arrows. Then work through the questions and exercises.

Work through the chapters from 1 to 11 in order. By doing this you will build on skills and understanding from one chapter to the next. By the end of the book you will have a good understanding of Year 3 English.

Good luck and have fun.

Jane Baker

Chapter 1 Writing a recount

A **recount** is a piece of writing that tells us about something that happened in the order that it happened.

STRUCTURE

LANGUAGE

Orientation who, when, where

Sequenced events what happened in the order that it happened

Conclusion ending, your personal comment

Our house removal

My Dad built a house on our farm. It wasn't our house. It was a house he built for a man in Bungendore.

When it was finished two men came to help us get the house ready to be moved. They cut the house into two halves with saws. Then they went away to have their lunch.

My friends Craig and Scott came to look at our house cut in two before it was towed away. They came because my Mum rang Mrs Smith and invited them. Craig and Scott were still there when the men came back late in the afternoon.

The men came back in two trucks. Both trucks were semi-trailers. The men brought two big two metre high jacks with them. One man, named Carl, switched on a little motor to make the jacks move up and down.

The house was about nine metres long. Each half was about three metres wide. The jacks lifted each half up high then the trucks backed under them. Carl switched the little motor on again and the jacks went down. When they stopped the two house halves were sitting on the backs of the semi-trailers.

After my Dad and the men made all the ropes tight the trucks took the house away. We watched it go up the hill and out the gate.

Now the house is in Bungendore and the man and his family live in it. I think they are happy in that house my Dad built.

Kevin (aged 7)

Facts about people and places

Time words to make order of events clearer

Interesting details

Verbs all in past tense

What did you read?

1. Who built the house? ______________________________

2. Where was the house built? ______________________________

3. Where is the house now? ______________________________

4. A crane loaded the house onto the trucks. **True or false?** ______________

5. Carl turned a handle to raise the jacks. **True or false?** ______________

6. **Circle** the names of Kevin's friends.
   a Scott b Carl c Craig

7. **Circle** the correct answer. The house WAS / WAS NOT moved in one piece.

8. Can you explain why the ropes had to be tight? ______________________________

____

How is it written?

1. The introduction tells us straight away what the recount is about. **True or false?** __________

2. **Circle** the one wrong answer. Kevin gives us the measurements of the house to:
   a show us how big the house was
   b show why two semi-trailers were needed
   c show off

3. Kevin tells us details of how things happened to make his recount more I __ T__ __ EST__ NG.

4. **Write** one interesting detail you learned from this recount about the way houses are moved.

____

____

5. **Circle** the right answer. The writer tells us what happened in:
   a any order b the order it happened

6. **Circle** the right answer. In the conclusion the writer tells us:
   a what happened to the house and what he thinks about it
   b what happened to the house

Spelling and meaning

half	calf	shelf	elf
halves	calves	shelves	elves

When you are learning to spell check for **spelling patterns** (e.g. elf → elves) then use the Look, Say, Cover, Write and Check method.

- **Look** hard at the word.
- **Say** the word out loud.
- **Cover** the word.
- **Write** the word on a piece of paper.
- **Check** your word against the printed word.

Do this again and again until you are sure of the word.

Learn the words in the word box using this method.

1 **Circle** the right word.

a Ali ate both halfs/halves of the apple.
b The elves/elfs stitched the shoemaker's boots overnight.
c The cow was very proud of her little red calve/calf.
d Those shelves/shelfs are dusty.

2 **Label** each picture correctly.

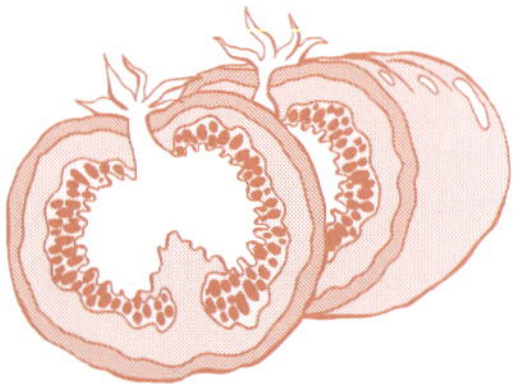

a ______________ b ______________ c ______________ d ______________

3 **Insert** a word from the word box in the spaces.

a Rabbits ate ______________ my father's lettuces last night.

b Paint those metal ______________ green to match the desks.

c Legends talk of mischievous little men called ______________.

d Baby horses are called foals and baby cows are called ______________.

e The two ______________ of the earth are called hemispheres.

Grammar

All sentences contain at least one complete idea and most sentences follow this pattern:
Someone/something → *doing* → *something*. We call this pattern **Subject** → **Verb** → **Object**.
Example **My Dad** (subject) **built** (verb) **a house** (object).

1. **Circle** the subject, **underline** the verb (doing word) and **draw a square** around the object.
   - a Edmund Hillary climbed Mount Everest.
   - b Snakes eat small birds.
   - c Storm clouds fill the sky.
   - d Mr Patel drives a removal truck.

2. Are these true sentences? Write **yes** or **no**.
   - a In the well. __________
   - b Lightning struck the old tree. __________
   - c Cyclone Tracy destroyed old Darwin. __________
   - d Over the mountain range. __________

3. **Complete** these five sentences by matching the objects to their subjects and verbs.

a	Five children played	peas and beans.
b	All our class plays	her good china.
c	Mrs Mercado packed	marbles.
d	A removal truck moved	soccer.
e	The gardener planted	our furniture.

Punctuation

All sentences start with a **capital letter**. Sentences that **tell** us something end with a **full stop**.
Example **T**rucks, buses and cars are all forms of transport**.**

Sentences that ask something end with a **question mark (?)**.

Example **I**s a ship a form of transport**?**

1. **Insert** a **full stop** or a **question mark** at the end of these sentences.
   - a Trucks with two trailers are called B-Doubles
   - b Does Mr Silvero drive a ute
   - c House-moving is very exciting

2. Help Josie punctuate her story. **Insert** all the **capital letters** and **full stops** and **question marks** that she has left out.

In the bush there are no traffic jams to worry drivers. instead drivers have to worry about dust. Why is this so big trucks leave great clouds of dust in the air and this makes it hard for drivers behind them to see where they are going

Fun with words

1 What am I? (The word box on page 4 will help you.)

a I have four legs, hooves and a long swishing tail. The sound I make rhymes with ZOO.

I am a ______________________.

b We are two flat, oblong pieces of wood set in a frame. We are friends with glasses, vases and books. We are ______________________.

c We wear little pointed caps and we like helping shoemakers at midnight.

We are ______________________.

d I'm what you get when you cut an apple into two equal parts. I am a ______________.

2 Do you know who we are? (We're not in the word box but your imagination will help you.)

a I'm green and I'm prickly. Farmers hate me but goats love to eat me. I am a T __ __ S __ LE.

b My legs are long and gangling. My tail is as long as my legs. My bed is a furry pocket that moves. I am a baby K __ __ G __ __ __ O. I am called a J __ __ Y.

3 These are all words to do with house-moving. Can you **unscramble** them?

a URNTIFURE ______________________ **b** OXBES ______________________

c RUCKT ______________________ **d** CKPA ______________________

e MOVALRE ______________________ **f** WRPA ______________________

4 Part of learning English is learning to speak clearly. **Practise** this tongue-twister.

Jack wanted to jack up the Jaguar with a big jack but John wanted the big jack to jack up the Jeep. Jack had to jack up the Jaguar with just a little jack, so John was joyful and Jack was not, when they were jacking up John's Jeep and Jack's Jaguar.

a **Time** yourself. **1** __________ minutes **2** __________ minutes **3** __________ minutes

b How quickly can you say it without getting mixed up? __________ minutes

Your turn to write

Tip for top writers

When you write a recount, make a plan before you start. First number the events in your recount according to the order in which they happen. Then write your recount in this order, starting with the first event and ending with the last.

1 Help Ben and Ivan recount their house removal by **numbering** their sentences in the correct order.

a wave goodbye ___	b pack boxes ___
c load furniture ___	d load boxes ___
e wake early ___	f drive away ___

2 **Write** your own recount of something exciting that has happened in your family by following the instructions.

a **List** all the events of your recount in the right order on the lines below.

b **Write** an **orientation** to start your recount.

c **Write** a **personal comment** to end your recount.

3 **Write** your **recount** on a separate piece of paper using the orientation, list of events and personal comment you have written above.

Chapter 2 Writing a narrative

A **narrative** tells a **story**. It can be a real story or an imaginary story.

STRUCTURE

LANGUAGE

Beach find

Orientation who, what, where, when

Fifteen years ago I was fishing in a boat with my dog Gruff. We were anchored off the beach when a big black fin cruised up beside us. It was a huge dolphin.

Complication sequence of events that make up the story

She whistled and clicked and told us, 'King Triton wants to see you'. Then she swallowed us.

We had a rough trip down to the ocean floor where we were spat out on the sand. There in front of us we saw the mighty King Triton. He barked some orders to a starfish who sped away.

Half an hour later the starfish returned. Behind him trailed other poor people and their dogs. They all had worried faces like ours. 'The king is about to make an announcement', hissed the starfish.

The king glared at us.

'Landcrabs,' he began. 'You will build me a house for every creature in my world, even the smallest of them.'

Resolution story ends

We are still building those houses, even after fifteen years. All we eat is seaweed and plankton.

Comment personal comment on what happened in the story

Before I put this in a bottle I must warn you:
Never, ever trust a dolphin.
Please help us.
Gruff and
Peter Small

Stephanie (aged 8)

Interesting verbs

Past tense all verbs in past tense

Direct speech exact words the character says

What did you read?

1. The title is 'Beach find'. What was found on the beach? ______________________

2. This story is about:
   a a dog b a boy and a dolphin c a request for rescue ______________________

3. How did the dolphin carry Gruff and Peter to the sea floor? ______________________

4. Who was King Triton's servant? ______________________

5. How do you think the other people and their dogs ended up in Triton's kingdom? ________

   ____

6. How long have Peter and Gruff been building houses for Triton? ______________________

7. a Did Triton feed his people? ______________

   b How do you know? ____

8. **Circle** the **wrong** answer.
   Peter put his message in a bottle:
   a to keep it dry b so it would float to shore c to use an unusual container

How is it written?

1. **Circle** the correct answer. The complication of the story is:
   a going fishing b the years of imprisonment c the chance of rescue

2. **Circle** the correct answer. Where the characters were and what they were doing at the time of capture is found in the:
   a orientation b complication c resolution

3. Stephanie has chosen her words carefully. She uses just one word to tell us that the prisoners walked slowly and unhappily. What is it? T __ __ __ __ ED

4. Direct speech (someone's own words) is a good way of letting someone in the story show what sort of a person they are. Triton calls his prisoners __ __ __ __ __ __ __ __. This word tells us he thinks he is very IMP __ __ T __ __ T and that he DOES/DOES NOT like people.

5. **Find** one example of direct speech from the text and write it here. ______________________

   ____

Spelling and meaning

anchor	dolphin	whistle	mighty
cruise	creature	trail	ocean
rough	seaweed	click	plankton

Remember the Look, Say, Cover, Write and Check way to spell.

1 **Draw** a sea picture in the box below. Include as many of the sea words in the word box as you can and write their names on them. Add any other sea words that you know to make it interesting.

2 **Match** the words in column A with their meanings in column B.

	A		B
a	plankton		any living animal or person
b	click		very tiny sea creatures
c	creature		sea between continents
d	ocean		sharp snapping sound

3 a –***ough*** is a common spelling for the sound –***uff***. Can you **complete** the table?

–*ough* word	Meaning
rough	not smooth
	strong
	sufficient

b –***ui*** is a common spelling for the sound –***oo***. Can you **complete** the table?

–*ui* word	Meaning
cruise	sail slowly
	apples and oranges
	when you bump your skin you can get this

Grammar

Writing is like building. It has tools and special ways to use them. Words are our tools. There are many kinds of words and each kind has a special use.
Some words are **naming** words. We call them **nouns**. Nouns name people and places and things and feelings.
Example When the ***ship*** sank the ***passengers*** took to the ***lifeboats***.

1 **Circle** the words that are nouns.

cupboard	sadness	pretty	horse	Australia
happy	paddock	church	walked	shop
ship	angry	round	climb	George

2 **Underline** all the nouns in these sentences.

- **a** Holidays are made of sun and sand and surf.
- **b** Flags on the beach show where it is safe to swim.
- **c** Seashells are the homes of tiny molluscs.
- **d** Starfish have bright red points along their five arms.
- **e** The tide rises and falls according to the moon.

3 **Write** beside all the things in the picture below the nouns that name them, including the parts of the dolphin (e.g. fin).

Punctuation

This writer was in a hurry and forgot to put in **capital letters** and **full stops**. Can you help? Remember each sentence starts with a capital, contains at least one idea and ends with a full stop.

when winter is past everyone is happy people wear sandals and sun hats children go swimming adults begin to garden again small plants grow tall and seeds turn into plants even birds are happy and busy building nests

Fun with words

1 Sea puzzles:

- **a** What has eight arms and swims? An O __ T __ P __ S
- **b** A dog's baby is a pup, so is a SH __ __ K'S and a S __ __ L'S.
- **c** A whale's baby, like a cow's, is called a C __ __ __.
- **d** A horse that has no legs and cannot lie down is a S __ __ HORSE.
- **e** A fish you might think a fighter is a S __ __ __ DFISH.
- **f** Did it fall from the sky into the sea? The S __ __ RFISH.

2 Answer the following and then write all the first letters in order on the line below to find the mystery word.

- **a** A container: __ __ X
- **b** A motor: __ NG __ N __
- **c** Very cross: __ N __ __ Y
- **d** A bear's baby: __ __ B
- **e** Not solid: __ O __ LOW
- **f** The mystery word is __ __ __ __ __. (Clue: I am washed by the surf.)

3 **a** The Great Barrier Reef puzzle: I grow like a plant and I look like a plant but I am really a tiny animal that likes to live in a heap with others like me. I am C __ R __ L.

b The Great Southern Ocean puzzle: I am the biggest animal in the world and the largest in my family. I only eat plankton because I have no teeth. I am the BLUE W __ __ LE.

4 Write the nouns in the box beside the parts of the ship they name.

anchor	mast	sail	bow	stern	deck	hull

Your turn to write

Tip for top writers

When you write a narrative try to include interesting information about people and places. This helps the reader to feel part of the story.

Imagine going fishing and having an adventure at the same time. **Write a story** about it in the space below.

These are some ideas that might help you. You do not have to use them if you have a story of your own all worked out.

- You fell out of the boat and had to be rescued.
- You caught a big silver fish.
- You saw a mermaid on the rocks.
- You met King Triton.
- The tide went out and you had to walk back over mudflats.

Title ______________________________

Orientation ______________________________

____

Complication ______________________________

____

____

____

____

____

____

____

____

____

____

____

Resolution ______________________________

____

Answers on pages 67–68

Chapter 3 Writing poetry

A **poem** is a word picture so clear that people can see and hear what the poet is writing about.

STRUCTURE

LANGUAGE

Rat

Brat rat,
pet rat,
my rat
in my hand.
On my shoulder
black and white,
beady eyes bright.
Dainty pink paws
pink shell ears,
pink snake tail,
always clean,
always fun,
just mine.
Curled inside
your warm green
drawer
till next time.

Kevin (aged 8)

Orientation introduces what poem is about

Description clear picture of rat

Conclusion ending (many poems do not have a conclusion)

Phrases not full sentences

Rhyming words

Comparisons to help us see their shape

Repetition

Interesting image (picture

What did you read?

1. **Circle** the correct answer. This poem is about:
   a a brat b a boy c a rat

2. The rat lives in a cage. **True or false?** ____________

3. How do we know this rat is not afraid of people? ______________________________

   ____

4. **Circle** the correct answer. ***Brat rat/pet rat*** tells us that this rat is:
   a always good b sometimes good c always bad

5. **Underline** the correct word. The rat has ROUND/OVAL eyes.

6. The rat sleeps lying straight. **True or false?** ____________

7. Does the rat's tail have fur on it? ____________

8. **Circle** the correct answer. Kevin's picture of his rat is:
   a a gentle picture b an angry picture c a cruel picture

How is it written?

1. Kevin's poem is not written in full sentences. It is written in phrases. **Write** the phrases Kevin used instead of saying ***My pet rat, that is sometimes a brat, is in my hand***.

   ____

   ____

2. ***Hand/band*** is an example of **rhyme**. Find two lines in the poem where the end words rhyme.

   ____

   ____

3. To tell us his rat has round ears the writer describes them as being like ____________.

4. To tell us the rat's tail is long and thin and round the writer describes it as being like a ____________.

5. **Circle** the correct answer. ***Dainty*** tells us the rat's paws are:
   a small and fine b small and sharp c small and ugly

6. **Circle three** correct answers. What feeling do we get from these lines?
   Curled inside
   your warm green
   drawer
   a safety b comfort c fear d unhappiness e contentment

Spelling and meaning

beady	dainty	bright
lead	paint	tight
beach	saint	sight
reach	faint	light

Each column in the word box follows a special **spelling pattern**. When you learn these words make sure you learn the pattern too. Patterns make learning new words easy.

1 **Complete** these sentences with words from the word box.

a Flotsam is something the sea has washed up on the ____________.

b If you look at the sun you will damage your ____________.

c Artists ____________ in oils and water colours.

d The ____________ of the moon fades as it grows smaller.

e Mrs Najif made the ____________ lace on that wedding dress.

2 **Choose** a word from the word box as a caption (label) for each of these pictures.

a ____________ b ____________ c ____________

3 Can you **make *–ea*** words to complete these sentences?

a Would you TEA __ __ me to play cards?

b Could you REA __ __ the jar on that shelf, please.

c Where is the dog's __ EAD? I want to take him for a walk.

4 a **Find** words from the word box to match these meanings:

ability to see ____________

not dark ____________

opposite of loose ____________

b Complete this sentence: The three words in 4a, above, share the __ __ __ __ spelling pattern.

Grammar

Adjectives are words that **describe** nouns. They tell us about colour, size, shape, age, feeling, taste, touch and sound. In fact they tell us all those things we know about through our senses.
Example A rat needs a ***warm***, ***safe*** house with plenty of ***fresh*** water.

1 **Underline** all the **adjectives** in these sentences.

a Seals have sleek, smooth brown fur and black eyes.
b Emus have long bare necks, strong legs and tiny useless wings.
c The house was old and shabby with crooked walls and chimney.
d Sweet-smelling sawdust makes a comfortable home for pet mice.
e In the empty park a sad boy searched for his lost dog.

Adjectives don't always come before a noun. Sometimes they stand alone after words like ***is***, ***are***, ***was*** and ***were***.
Example The new pups are ***black*** and ***white***.

2 **Underline** all the **adjectives** in these sentences.

a New foals and calves are always clumsy.
b Inoki was always happy watching tropical fish in the glass tank.
c Kate, Mira and Selena were all in the same class and never lonely.
d Rough play can frighten a dog into becoming a bad-tempered dog.
e Green tree snakes make gentle pets.

Sometimes we can make adjectives out of nouns. A common ending for an adjective is ***–y***.
Example ***bead → beady***

3 Can you **make adjectives** out of these nouns? Be careful of the last three.

Noun	Adjective	Noun	Adjective
a leaf		b sand	
c dirt		d anger	
e hunger		f friend	

Punctuation

We use a **comma (,)** to separate a group of adjectives from each other.
Example The common garden mouse is a ***quick, small, grey*** thief of food scraps.

Insert all the missing commas in the following sentences.

a Seal pups are fat round roly-poly balls of soft fur.
b Magpies build big strong nests high up off the ground.

c Crimson rosellas flash scarlet blue and green in flight.

d Keeping pets is an interesting enjoyable and responsible hobby.

Fun with words

eagle rat mouse frog snake guinea pig magpie goldfish wombat dog python lizard cat whale penguin canary budgerigar dingo

1 Can you **sort** the words in the box into the right columns? (The first is done for you.)

Scales	Fur	Feathers	Skin
		eagle	

2 Most animal homes have a name (e.g. a bird has a nest). Can you **match** these animals to their homes?

a pig		stable
b horse		burrow
c rabbit		colony
d fox		stye
e seal		den

3 There are special names for people who work with animals too. Using the words in the net can you **name** these people?

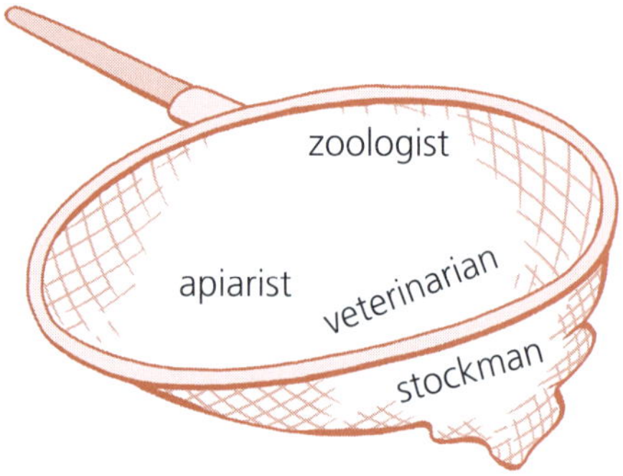

a I study animal behaviour: Z __ __ L __ G __ ST

b I look after bees: AP __ __ RIST

c I look after cattle and sheep: ST __ __ KM __ N

d I look after sick animals: V __ __ ER __ NARI __ N

4 Following the pattern ***ring is to finger as sock is to shoe,*** **complete** the following associations. You have been given a clue to each of the answers.

a Scales are to fish as F __ __ is to cats.

b Wool is to sheep as F __ __ __ __ __ __ __ are to birds.

c Web is to spider as B _ _ _ _ _ is to rabbit.

d Beak is to hen as B _ _ _ is to duck.

e Sky is to eagle as O _ _ _ _ is to whale.

f Claws are to birds as H _ _ _ _ _ are to horses.

Your turn to write

Tip for top writers

The best poetry sounds like singing. Good poets:

- often use **short phrases** instead of full sentences
- choose their **adjectives** carefully
- use **rhyming** words
- **repeat** words and phrases

1 Kevin wrote about his rat:

pink shell ears,
pink snake tail.

Think about the shapes and colours of these animals and to what you might compare them. Then **write two lines** that let us see your animal clearly.

Pig	Dog
____________________	____________________
____________________	____________________

2 Another way of writing a poem about an animal is to **list** everything you know about it in single words. Read the two examples and then write two yourself.

Soft	Hissing	__________	__________
silent	spitting	__________	__________
green-eyed	yowling	__________	__________
curled	clawing	__________	__________
content	scratching	__________	__________
CAT	CAT	__________	__________

3 Now that you have practised writing poetry, try writing a poem all by yourself about any animal you like. Use a separate piece of paper.

Chapter 4 Writing an information report

An **information report** is a piece of writing that informs the reader. Reports only contain **facts**. They do not include opinion (what the writer thinks).

STRUCTURE

LANGUAGE

Life cycle of the butterfly

Introduction usually includes a definition

Butterflies are caterpillars when they are born. All caterpillars become moths or butterflies unless something happens to them first.

All fact, no opinion

Organised information new paragraph for each new development

1. Their lives progress through different stages. Firstly the butterfly eggs lie on the leaves of plants where their mother laid them. Next the eggs hatch and little caterpillars climb out.

Technical words

2. The caterpillar eats and eats. It eats leaves and grows fat.

3. Soon the caterpillar builds a large cocoon around itself. It stays inside that cocoon for more than two weeks.

4. Finally, the cocoon splits and the new beautiful butterfly emerges. It sits in the sun till its wings are dry and strong. Then it flies away to sit on flowers and collect pollen. When it flies from flower to flower it mixes different pollens and helps more flowers to grow.

Present tense all verbs in present tense

Anthea (aged 8)

What did you read?

1. **Circle** the correct answer. The life cycle of a butterfly starts when it is:

   a a caterpillar

   b an egg

   c a butterfly

2. What hatches out of the egg? ____________________

3. What does the caterpillar eat? ____________________

4. When it has grown big and fat what does the caterpillar do?

   ____

5. **Circle** the correct answer. The cocoon is used as:

   a a shelter b a box for food c to make silk

6. The new butterfly waits for its wings to __ __ __ before it flies.

7. Why does the butterfly visit flowers? ______________________________

How is it written?

1. A report tells us facts about something. **Write** two facts that you find in the first paragraph.

   ____

   ____

2. A report uses technical words. **Find** the technical words in this report that mean:

   a what an egg does to produce new life: __ __ __ __ __

   b the fertile yellow dust at the centre of a flower: __ __ __ __ __ __

3. **Circle** the correct answer. Sometimes a report is followed by a diagram. Anthea's diagram shows:

   a a cocoon

   b the life cycle of a butterfly

4. **Circle** the correct answer. The diagram gives the same information as the report:

   a to fill up space

   b to add interest to the report

   c to illustrate the connections between the facts in the report

Spelling and meaning

butterfly	different	hatch	leaves
caterpillar	stage	collect	beautiful
pollen	build	cocoon	emerge

1 **Insert** a word from the list in each of the spaces.

a Bees, like butterflies, gather ____________ from flowers.

b The ____________ of some trees turn scarlet and gold in autumn.

c John was as snug in his bed as a caterpillar in its ____________.

d Ducks and hens sit on their eggs until they ___________.

2 English has many words that mean the same thing. We call these words **synonyms**. **Match** the words in **A** with words in **B** that mean the same.

A		B
a different		gather
b collect		period
c stage		lovely
d beautiful		unlike

3 Plural means more than one. **Write the plurals** of these words.

a caterpillar: ______________ b cocoon: ______________

4 Most **plurals** end in *–s*. Words ending in *–y* change the *–y* to *–ies* in the plural (e.g. butterfly → butterflies). **Make plurals** out of these words.

spy ____________________ fly ____________________ sky ____________________

5 Most words ending in *–f* change *–f* to *–ves* in the plural (e.g. leaf → leaves). **Make plurals** out of these words.

hoof ____________________ calf ____________________ elf ____________________

6 Write the **plural** forms of the following words.

school __________________ shelf __________________ house __________________

horse __________________ baby __________________ dinghy __________________

Grammar

Another valuable tool for writers is the **verb**. A verb is a word that says something or does something.

Examples Peter ***talked*** to our class.
Meteorologists ***study*** weather patterns.

A verb can also be a word that tells us something is alive or can be found in a particular place.

Examples A butterfly ***is*** a beautiful insect.
In that tree ***is*** a beehive.

1 **Underline** all the **verbs** in these sentences.

a Tadpoles grow into frogs.

b Ducklings and chickens hatch out of eggs.

c The taipan is Australia's most venomous snake.

d Monarch butterflies are orange and black and travel in groups of a thousand or more.

e Baby turtles hatch from eggs in the sand, then scramble across the beach, dive into the water and swim out to sea.

Information reports are usually written as if they are happening now. We call this writing in the **present tense**. We know the tense from the verb in the sentence.
Example Kangaroos ***carry*** their babies in a pouch.

2 Write these sentences in the present tense by **changing the verb**.

a Blue-ringed octopuses lived in rockpools.

___

b Funnel-web spiders trapped insects in sticky webs around their hole.

___

c The magpie began life as an egg, hatched into a fledgling and then grew into an adult bird.

___

___

3 Look at Mele's report below. **Underline** all the verbs and then **circle** the sentence that is **not** in the present tense.

Kangaroos are marsupials. Like all marsupials they raise their babies in a pouch. The pouch was warm and soft. It is comfortable and safe for the baby joeys.

Punctuation

When we **list** things (names, actions) we separate them all with a **comma**.
Example Many animals only live in Australia. Some of these are koalas**,** kangaroos**,** wombats**,** platypuses and echidnas.

Insert all the missing commas.

Lions tigers jaguars cheetahs and the common house cat all belong to the same family, the feline family. Wolves dingoes and jackals are all relatives of our pet dogs.

Fun with words

1. Think about your life. Then on a separate piece of paper **draw** a careful life cycle diagram to illustrate your life through all its stages from baby to old person. Draw an arrow from one stage to the next and label each stage (e.g. birth → baby → pre-school).

2. People and animals are alike in lots of ways. In English we have many animal sayings to describe something well known about a person. **Match** the sayings in A to the right person in B.

A		B
a as lazy as a pig in mud		thinks he/she is special
b as silly as a wet hen		is not to be trusted
c as hungry as a horse		won't work
d as sly as a fox		is very strong
e as strong as an ox		isn't sensible
f as vain as a peacock		hasn't eaten

3. See if you can **make up** some new animal sayings to describe these people.

   a a very noisy person → as noisy as a ____________

   b a very busy person → as busy as a ____________

   c a very fast runner → as fast as a ____________

4. We like to explain things with a **definition** (e.g. An octopus is an eight-armed sea creature.) Here are some funny definitions that can be **completed** with words from the box below. You will not need all the words.

   a A ________________ is a lot of holes tied up with string.

   b A ________________ is a collection of leaves that do not grow on trees.

   c An ________________ is a small machine for waking people who do not have a rooster.

shoe	net	book	bird	alarm clock

Your turn to write

Tip for top writers

When you write an information report:

- write in the present tense
- keep your facts in order

Here are some facts about fairy penguins. Using these facts **write** a report on fairy penguins for your class.

A fairy penguin:

- is a small marine bird
- has very small wings for swimming
- cannot fly
- lives in the waters of southern Australia
- mostly nests on islands
- goes fishing during the day
- returns at night with food for babies
- nests with other fairy penguins in colonies called rookeries (most famous Australian rookery is on Phillip Island in Victoria)

FAIRY PENGUINS

Orientation ______________________________

____

Information (arranged in paragraphs of facts) ______________________________

____

____

____

____

____

____

____

____

____

____

Chapter 5 Writing a description of a person

A **description** of a person is a piece of writing that lets us know that person as well as the writer does.

STRUCTURE

LANGUAGE

The fisherman

Mr Lee was a quiet man. He rarely spoke. A smile and a nod were what we shared. He was mending a net when I first saw him. Squatting on his heels, he was rapidly passing a green net through his fingers. Every so often he stopped to patch a tear or strengthen a weak section that might break under the strain of the good catch he dreamed about.

Every day, an hour before the tide turned, Mr Lee would appear from among the palm trees that grew down to the beach. He wore a faded blue shirt, ragged shorts and an old rice-straw hat that almost hid his face. That is probably why I noticed his hands first. For a small, thin man he had big, strong hands. They were hands that could mend a net and cast it, hour after hour, out over the sea.

When his net was ready for the day's work Mr Lee would wade out into the sea. Standing knee-deep he would grasp the net evenly between his hands and, in a single graceful movement, cast it out over the water.

Sometimes he would hum quietly to himself. Mostly he didn't. He cast his net, pulled it back and cast it again. He was at home in the sea and the sunlight. He was content.

When the sun sank low and the sea darkened he would gather his net and set off back up the beach. Under the trees he prepared his catch of silver fish for sale in the night market. Then he disappeared into the darkness.

Kitty Carrera

Introduction
- man introduced in first sentence
- his work

Description
- his clothing
- his hands
- his day
- his mood

Conclusion
end of his day

Verbs all in same tense this writer uses past tense

Carefully chosen adjectives so reader can see his clothes

Adverbs to show *how* action is done

What did you read?

1 **Circle** the correct answer. Mr Lee was a:

a net maker b fisherman c beach inspector

2 He wore a faded green shirt. **True or false?** __________

3 His hat was made out of ________________.

4 **Circle** the correct answer. He fished from:

a a boat b the beach c shallow water

5 Mr Lee was small and thin. **True or false?** _______________

6 We know Mr Lee lived in a warm tropical place because the trees are ___________ trees.

7 a Do you think Mr Lee was a rich man? _______________________

b Why do you think so? ____

____

How is it written?

1 What word in the first sentence tells us that Mr Lee did not speak very often? _______________

2 Writers always try to use the most exact words they can. In paragraph 3 what words has this writer used to mean:

a walk through water: ____________ b throw a net: ____________

3 Adjectives give detail and interest to descriptions. From paragraph 2 **write down** the adjectives that describe Mr Lee's clothes. ____

4 A description can tell us about personality by telling us how a person does something. **Circle** the correct answer. ***Sometimes he would hum quietly to himself.*** This tells us Mr Lee was:

a happy b bored c lonely

5 Sometimes a writer can tell us something indirectly. ***The sun sank low*** tells us the time of day was SUN __ __ T.

6 In describing the fisherman the writer referred to his:

a CL __ __ __ ING b H __ __ DS

c DAY'S W __ __ K d M __ __ D

7 **Circle** the correct answer. A description always keeps the same tense from start to finish. This description is written in the PAST/PRESENT tense.

Spelling and meaning

quiet	strengthen	stop	tap
rarely	knee	stopped	tapped
shoulder	knife	gracefully	rapidly

Silent letters are letters that we do not say.
Example the ***k*** in ***knee***
Be careful with these.

1 a **Write** one word (not from the word box) under each of these pictures to explain it.

______________ ______________ ______________

b **Circle** the word that does not include a silent letter.

2 **Replace** the underlined words with words from the word box.

a We don't very often eat lollies. ______________

b The baby is not making a sound. ______________

c Muscles get strong with exercise. ______________

d Ballet dancers move with grace. ______________

Vowels (the letters ***a***, ***e***, ***i***, ***o*** and ***u***) can be pronounced short or long.
Example tap (short) tape (long)
This can change a word's meaning. We know to pronounce the middle vowel long if the word ends in the letter ***e***. We call this **bossy *e*** because it bosses the vowels around.

3 **Circle** the right word.
a Kangaroos can hop/hope very fast.
b Grapes are grown on the slop/slope of a hill.
c Will you mop/mope the floor, please.

4 Using the sto**p/**sto**pped** spelling pattern **make new words** out of the following.

mop ______	hop ______	sip ______
top ______	sop ______	rip ______
tap ______	sap ______	tip ______

Grammar

When we write about things that happened in the past we call this writing in the **past tense**. The verb tells us what tense is being used.

Examples The postman **stops** at every letterbox. **(present tense)**
The postman **stopped** at every letterbox. **(past tense)**

1 **Change** to past tense by changing the underlined verb.

a My dad <u>mops</u> out the garage on Saturday. ____________________

b Eddie <u>sops</u> up the spilt milk with his handkerchief. ____________________

c Willy Ollilla <u>tops</u> the goal chart every season. ____________________

d Surveyors <u>map</u> Australia from the air. ____________________

2 Sam has confused his present and past tenses. Can you help him? **Rewrite** his sentences so that they are all in the **past tense**.

a The Titanic sank when it collides with an iceberg in 1912.

____

b Pemulwuy is a brave Aboriginal warrior who lived around Sydney Harbour in the late 1700s.

____

c When night falls bats came out of their cave.

____

Punctuation—Revision

1 **Insert capitals** and **full stops** to separate these sentences.

in Australia many people enjoy fishing one of the most dangerous ways to fish is to fish from rocks at the bottom of a cliff big waves often sweep rockfishers into the sea where many drown

2 **Insert** the missing **commas**.

a Yabbies prawns lobsters crabs and Moreton Bay bugs all belong to the family of crustaceans.

b Geordie's favourite T-shirt is a holey old red green and blue striped shirt that was given to him when he was six.

c The Lachlan Murray Murrumbidgee and Darling river system is the largest in Australia.

d To own a dog you must feed it train it walk it brush it and love it.

Fun with words

Some words are **counting** words and others are **weighing** words. It is important not to confuse them.
Many and ***few*** are **counting** words.
Much and ***less*** are **weighing** words.
Examples Ali has ***many*** marbles but Ricky has only a ***few***.
Is there ***much*** more flour than sugar? Yes, but there is ***less*** salt than flour.
(You can count marbles but you can't count flour, sugar or salt. You can only heap it up and weigh it.)
More is both a **counting** and a **weighing** word.
Example Mrs Jones sells ***more*** material and buttons than knitting wool and needles.

1 **Sort** the words from the box into the right bins.

needles rakes sugar wheat cans letters powder ice-cream ice-blocks custard rice gravy jelly pumpkins trees pepper apples gates trucks soup jam

Counting bin

Weighing bin

2 A good way of describing things is to compare them to something else (e.g. The class room was a busy as a hive of bees). What do you think these could be **compared to**?

a a crowded school bus: ______________________

b lots of people running in different directions: ______________________

c a rainbow in the sky: ______________________

JOKE

Q. When were there only three vowels in the alphabet?
A. Before **U** and **I** were born.

Your turn to write

Tip for top writers

Descriptions are word pictures. Pretend you are an artist and paint a picture with words of colour, shape, size and mood.

1. Year 3 at Bunyip Primary School has given us a table of facts about their teacher, Mr Polly. **Read** them carefully and then **write** a description of Mr Polly.

Is	Has	Does	Can	Wears
tall	long fingers	laughs a lot	be cross	blue shirts
thin	a jolly voice	tells jokes	be very kind	terrible yellow ties
about 40	black hair	plays the piano	sing	grey trousers
strict about homework	olive skin	helps students in trouble	draw dragons	glasses

2. **Think** carefully about your best friend. Think about height and hair colour, likes and dislikes, eyes and size, personality and appearance; think about how you first met, what you liked about your friend at that first meeting, what you play together and so on.
Then **write** a description of your best friend. Use your own paper for this writing.

Answers on pages 69–70

Chapter 6 Giving your opinion in a speech

An **opinion speech** tells the audience what the speaker thinks about something and tries to persuade them to agree with him or her.

STRUCTURE

LANGUAGE

Learning to swim

Opinion all children should learn to swim

All children must learn how to swim. There are many reasons for this. It's fun and it gives you lots of exercise. The most important reason for learning to swim is that it saves people from drowning.

Argument reasons for learning to swim

Firstly, swimming stops many children from drowning. If a child gets caught in a rip he can swim out of it. If he can't swim he will most likely drown. In the bush some children drown when they fall into dams and they cannot swim. Other children walk into deep creeks and drown. If they could all swim no one would drown.

Secondly, swimming makes children stronger and healthier. It makes muscles work and get strong. Children get a bit of fresh air in their lungs too when they are in the water away from the classroom.

Finally, swimming means you don't just have to play at the edge of the water and on the sand. You can dive straight in and play other sorts of games, like catching waves.

Conclusion repeats opinion

I think it's a very good idea for everyone to learn to swim, don't you?

Anthea (aged 8)

Example makes argument believable

Numbering connects arguments and helps audience understand

Talks directly to audience

Question involves audience

What did you read?

1. What is the most important reason for learning to swim?

____

2. Give one other reason offered by Anthea for learning to swim.

____

3. **Circle** the right answer. What happens when you are caught in a rip?

   a You are swept out to sea.
   b Your swimming costume is ripped.
   c You are dumped on the beach.

4. **Circle** the best answer. A dam is:

   a a lake
   b a pond made by people
   c a billabong

5. **Complete** this sentence. Swimming makes your __________ strong and puts __________ __________ in your lungs.

6. What sort of games do you think you could play in the sand at the water's edge?

____

____

7. **Circle** the right answer. ***catching a wave*** means:

   a filling a bucket with sea water
   b touching a wave
   c swimming on a wave to the shore

How is it written?

1. What is the first sentence of the speech? __________________________

2. What is the last sentence of the speech? __________________________

3. These two sentences are almost the same. Why? **Circle** the correct answer.

   a Anthea is reminding her audience of the point of her speech.
   b Anthea has run out of ideas.
   c Anthea likes repeating things.

4. **Circle** the correct answer. The reasons are arranged by number:

   a so the speaker won't forget them
   b to sound intelligent
   c to help the audience remember the arguments

5. **Circle** the right answer. When the speaker says ***I think*** this suggests that she is:

   a unsure of her facts
   b sincere
   c vain

Spelling and meaning

drown	town	edge	dredge
frown	down	ledge	hedge
learn	likely	straight	finally

1 Can you **write** all the words in the top two lines in alphabetical order? Remember, if the first letters are the same look at the **second letter** to decide which word comes before the other in the alphabet.

_______________ _______________ _______________ _______________

_______________ _______________ _______________ _______________

2 **Complete** these sentences with words from the word box.

a Eagles like to nest on a ___________ on the face of a cliff.

b A thorny ___________ is a safe nesting place for sparrows.

c A ___________ wrinkled his forehead.

d That line is not ___________, it is curved.

e Those clouds suggest it is ___________ to rain today.

3 Can you **make** ***–edge*** and ***–ow*** words meaning:

a a promise: P __ EDGE

b a female pig: __ OW

c a disagreement: __ OW

d a drying cloth: __ OW __ L

e a light rainfall: __ __ OW __ R

f a bear's angry voice: G __ OW __

4 **Match** the words in **A** to their meanings in **B**.

	A		B
a	likely		large village
b	hedge		a river-cleaning barge
c	straight		probable
d	dredge		a close row of shrubs
e	town		without curves

Grammar

We know that nouns are words that name things. Two kinds of nouns are common nouns and proper nouns.

Common nouns are general names.

Examples ***country***, ***child***, ***doctor***

Proper nouns are special names or titles that belong to one thing or one person. Proper nouns always start with a capital letter.

Examples ***India***, ***Julie***, ***Doctor Habib***

1 **Underline** all the proper nouns in this passage.

Cathy Freeman is one of Australia's most famous female athletes. She won medals in three Olympic Games. Cathy lit the torch at the Olympics in Sydney in 2000 as well as winning gold.

2 **Circle** the common nouns and **underline** all the proper nouns in these sentences.

- **a** Many famous sportspeople are Aboriginals, including runner Cathy Freeman, AFL player Gavin Wanganeen and Rugby League player Mal Meninga.
- **b** One of our most popular pastimes is swimming. For three months, from December till the end of February, the pools are crowded.
- **c** There are twelve months in a year and three months in every season, with December to February being summer and June to August, winter.

3 The following are all common nouns. Can you write down a **proper noun** related to it (e.g. river → Yarra River).

Common noun	Proper noun
a building	
b country	
c bridge	
d man	
e school	

Punctuation

This passage has lost many of its **capital letters**. Can you **replace** them?

waltzing matilda is australia's most famous song. it was written by andrew barton paterson more than a century ago. at the time paterson was visiting dagworth station near winton in queensland. waltzing matilda was sung in public for the first time on 6 april 1895.

Fun with words

Words can be used to mean things that, at first glance, seem to have nothing to do with each other.

Examples Sam's father works in an opal **mine**.
Mr O'Donnell is a **mine** of information about rivers.

(If you think about it, the connection is that mines contain lots of things people want. People who want to know all about rivers will find all their answers by asking Mr O'Donnell because he knows so much about rivers.)

1 What words in the word box on page 34 would work in these sentence pairs?

a My bangle fell ____________ the well. I feel very ____________ because my budgie is sick.

b Many rock fishers have __ __ __ __ __ ED in the sea. I got __ __ __ __ __ ED in that storm.

c A margin is a ____________ line down the edge of a page. He sat ____________ down to work without fooling around.

2 When we make a speech we address the people we are talking to by title. Can you **match** these titles and terms of address to their audiences?

Term of address		Audience
a Ladies and Gentlemen		children in your class
b Fellow students		member of parliament
c The Honourable Mr		group of grown-ups

3 Swimming is an aquatic sport, a sport played in water. The word ***aquatic*** comes from an old Latin word *aqua*, which means water.

a Can you think of three other aquatic sports?

____________ ____________ ____________

b What is the name of a zoo that only contains fish and other sea creatures?

AQUA __ __ UM

4 Puzzle: I live on the sea floor. I am always moving but stay in the same place. I grow but I do not eat anything. I am green and brown and cold and wet. Little fish live in my hair. What am I? I am S __ __ __ __ __ D

Your turn to write

Tip for top writers

A good speech **begins** and **ends** with the **main** idea so the audience will remember it.

1. Imagine you were asked to persuade your school principal to allow your class to visit the zoo. **Write**, in order of importance, the points you would make to convince the principal.

   1

   2

   3

   4

   5

2. Now write the speech you would make using the points you have written above.

Orientation

Point 1

Point 2

Point 3

Point 4

Point 5

Conclusion

Chapter 7 Writing to persuade: advertisement

When we write to persuade we are trying to convince the reader to do something. An **advertisement** is written to **persuade** the reader to **buy** something.

STRUCTURE

- ***Title*** name of what is being advertised
- ***Location*** where sale to be held
- ***Details of goods for sale***
- ***Necessary information*** date, time and place

LANGUAGE

- ***Capital letters*** to catch attention for important words
- ***Short phrases*** very few complete sentences in thi advertisement
- ***Exclamation marks*** to suggest how amazingly gooc the sale is
- ***Words*** to suggest price is cheap
- ***Talks directly*** to reader

ANNUAL JUNE SALE

TERRIFIC TOYS

Red-hot Bargains!

Fantastic Specials!

Every day till sold out!

BMX bikes at never before low prices!

Remote control cars cheaper than you could believe!

IMAGINE

baby dolls from only $19.99

board games just $12.99

Be the coolest kid on the block with a **Sandman skateboard** at just $39.95

DON'T MISS IT!

Be first in line when the doors open
Monday 16 June at 9 am

Terrific Toys
56 Prickle Street
Spikey Plains

What did you read?

1. How often is this sale held? ______________________________

2. When will the sale begin? ______________________________

3. When will it end? ______________________________

4. How much will a board game cost? ______________________________

5. All baby dolls will cost $19.99. **True or false?** ____________

6. **Circle** the correct answer. The business holding the sale is:

   a Terrific Toys

   b Spikey Plains Toy Shop

   c Sandman Toys

7. **Circle** the correct answer. What does Terrific Toys want you to do when you read this advertisement?

   a look at toys

   b buy toys

   c get up early on Monday

How is it written?

1. **Circle** the correct answer. This kind of writing:

   a describes a sale
   b tells a story about a sale
   c persuades you to go to a sale

2. **Circle** the correct answer. There are many QUESTION/EXCLAMATION marks in the punctuation of this advertisement.

3. **Circle** the correct answer. The use of this punctuation mark is meant to make you feel:

   a surprise   b excitement   c fear

4. **Circle** the one **wrong** answer. The words ***bargain*** and ***special*** tell us the goods on sale are:

   a not well made   b cheap   c specially priced for sale

5. **Complete** these words in the advertisement that tell us the prices are very, very, cheap:

   F __ __ __ __ __ __ __ C and R __ __ -H __ __ .

Spelling and meaning

annual	bargain	fantastic	cheap
sale	special	remote	terrific
sail	believe	control	imagine

Be careful with words that end in ***-ic / -ick***. Most adjectives that end with this sound have the spelling ***-ic*** (e.g. ***terrific*** and ***fantastic***) but some use ***-ick*** (e.g. ***sick***). Most nouns are spelt -***ick*** but a few end with ***-ic*** (e.g. ***elastic***).

1. Can you **spell** these words?

   a Something used to build a house: B __ __ __ __

   b A thin rod of wood: ST __ __ __

   c Very horrible: HORRIF __ __

   d Thin stretchy material: ELAST __ __

   e Not well: S __ __ __

2. **Insert** a word from the word box in the spaces.

   a Christmas is an ____________ holiday in Australia and New Zealand.

   b Do you __________ in fairies?

   c If I close my eyes I can ___________ I am flying like a bird.

   d To change channels on the television I use the __________.

To use ***a*** (a cat) and ***an*** (an egg) correctly look at the word that follows it.
Rule: Use ***an*** before a vowel (a, e, i, o, u), ***a*** before consonants (every other letter).

3. **Insert *a*** or ***an*** in each of the spaces.

   a He ate ___ apple but not ___ banana.

   b ___ orangutan is ___ red-haired member of the ape family.

   c That blade does not have ___ edge. It is blunt.

4. **Complete** this sentence by inserting ***a*** and ***an*** where necessary.

   Id al Fitr, like Christmas, is ___ annual celebration. Muslims celebrate it with ___ feast just as Christians celebrate Christmas with ___ feast.

Grammar

In some kinds of writing (e.g. in poetry and advertisements), we often use phrases instead of sentences. A **phrase** is a group of words without a verb.
Examples Red hot bargains   Annual June Sale

1 **Write S** (sentence) or **P** (phrase) at the end of each of the following.

a John wants to sell his skateboard. ______

b Unbeatable prices! ______

c before the end of March ______

d on the top shelf ______

e Compare prices before you buy. ______

Adverbs tell us how, when and where something is done.
Examples Pham ran ***quickly*** to the letterbox. (how)
It is best to eat ***after*** swimming, not ***before***. (when)
Kangaroos are grazing over ***there*** on the hill. (where)

2 **Circle** all the adverbs in these sentences.

a The book sale will begin tomorrow.
b Music played and little flags fluttered overhead at the fete.
c The shoppers trudged wearily homeward.
d Advertisements for the bonfire night must be sent today.
e Breezes gently shifted the leaves of the old gum tree.

3 Adverbs are often used in phrases. **Underline** the adverb in each of these phrases.

a over here

b on sale tomorrow

c fantastic prices everywhere

d bright sunlight overhead

e after the party

Punctuation

When we exclaim we are showing surprise, excitement or alarm in our voices. To show this in writing we use an **exclamation mark (!)**.
Examples Ouch**!** Fantastic**!** Watch out**!**
We also use an exclamation mark to show a sudden loud noise.
Examples Bang**!** Crash**!** Thump**!**

Insert an exclamation mark after the words that show strong feelings like surprise, excitement or alarm.

1 Bang The balloon burst and scared us all.

2 Screech The brakes locked tight and the car skidded.

3 Help Help was the cry from inside the jammed lift.

4 Penny and Nijmeh read the warning: Danger No Swimming.

Fun with words

Many years ago a sweets-maker invented a new lolly and gave it a wonderful name to describe what it was, how delicious it was and how happy it would make people. That name was Lollygobbleblissbomb (it's true—ask your grandparents). The new sweet was a best seller in the lolly shops.

1 Can you **invent** names for these things, names so special people will want to rush out and buy them.

a a sticky, chewy, nutty lolly on a stick ______________________

b a tiny one-person car with no doors, only a lift-up lid ______________________

c a fluffy pink toy pig that grunts and trots ______________________

2 ***Annual*** events happen only once a year. **Write** down the names of at least three annual events you know of (don't forget your own birthday).

a ______________________________________

b ______________________________________

c ______________________________________

3 a The Olympic Games are an annual event. **True or false?** __________

b Ramadan and Easter occur annually. **True or false?** __________

c Chinese New Year occurs annually. **True or false?** __________

4 You want to sell the following things. Can you think of good persuasive words to describe each one in an advertisement? **Write** at least two persuasive words under each picture.

______________ ______________ ______________ ______________

______________ ______________ ______________ ______________

Your turn to write

Tip for top writers

When you write an advertisement:

- Keep it short.
- Use exciting words.
- Include details of time, place and price.

1. One Tree School is going to hold a bonfire night. **Write** an advertisement in the box persuading people to come.

   Make sure you **include**:

   - where it will be held
   - when it will begin
   - how much it will cost

2. **Imagine** you have been asked to write the advertisement for the Lollygobbleblissbomb to persuade people to taste it and buy it. **Write** that advertisement in the box. Include colours and pictures to make your advertisement look attractive.

Chapter 8 Writing a procedure

A **procedure** is a piece of writing that tells someone what to do or how to do it.

Alex is a new student at Williga Central School. The principal has asked John to help make Alex welcome. He gave John the following instructions so the two boys can meet and walk to school together.

STRUCTURE

LANGUAGE

Aim

Walking to school with Alex

Walking instructions in order that John should follow them

Each instruction begins with a verb and is written as a command

1 Walk down Cave Road to Hill Street.

2 Turn left into Hill Street.

3 Walk about 50 metres along Hill Street then cross the road into Shady Lane.

4 Meet Alex on the corner at the end of Shady Lane.

5 Walk down the hill along Gumnut Drive.

6 Continue along the river, over the creek at Buckley's Crossing and up the hill.

7 Turn left into Boronia Road and then into our school.

Exact details including names and measurements

Special instructions

Don't forget to walk in single file over Buckley's Crossing. It is narrow and dangerous.

Explanation for previous instruction

I will expect you at my office at 9 am.

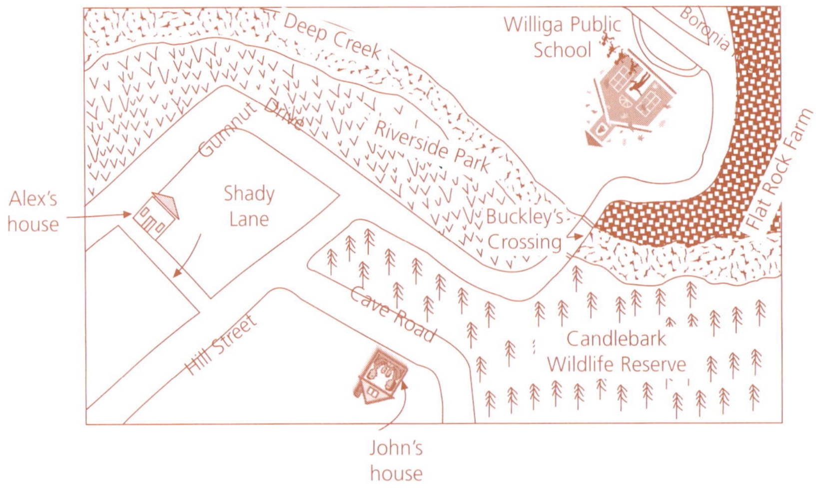

What did you read?

1. **Circle** the correct answer. The principal gave John these instructions so:

   a he can find Alex's house
   b he will cross the creek safely
   c he can walk to school with Alex

2. Alex lives in Boronia Road. **True or false?** ____________

3. **Circle** the correct answer. Who lives in Hill Street?

   a Alex b John c nobody

4. When John walks down Cave Road, does he turn right or left into Hill Street? ____________

5. Why must the boys walk in single file over Buckley's Crossing?

   ____

6. Following the instructions, draw the route to school on the map.

How is it written?

1. **Circle** the correct answer. What sort of writing is this?

   a a story
   b a set of instructions
   c a description of a town called Williga

2. **Circle** the correct answer. These instructions are written as:

   a commands b questions c simple sentences

3. **Circle** the correct answer. The first word in each instruction is:

   a a noun b a verb
   c an adjective d an adverb

4. **Circle** the correct answer. The instructions are numbered:

   a to make them clearly understandable
   b to save time
   c to look important

5. **Circle** the two **wrong** answers. These instructions include:

   a street directions
   b a warning
   c details about Flat Rock farm
   d house location
   e an appointment time

Spelling and meaning

instruction	welcome	race	face
follow	election	racing	facing
correction	dangerous	direction	narrow

Spelling rule: Words that end in –***ce*** drop the –***e*** when you add –***ing***.

1 Following this rule **add *ing*** to these words.

a pace ______________

b lace ______________

c dice ______________

d ice ______________

e trace ______________

2 **Choose** words from the word box to fill the spaces.

a Only bikes can go down that lane. It is too ______________ for cars.

b Deep water is ______________ for non-swimmers.

c '______________ home', said Lucy's mother on her return.

d ______________ these instructions carefully.

3 **Match** the words in **A** to their meanings in **B**.

A		B
a correction		north, south, east, west
b direction		not wide
c narrow		making right
d instruction		telling how

4 Words that are **opposite** in meaning are called **antonyms**. **Match** these words with their antonyms.

Word		Antonym
a dangerous		unwelcome
b follow		safe
c narrow		lead
d welcome		wide

5

These caterpillars are crawling in S _ _ _ _ _ F _ _ _ .

Grammar

Instructions are **always** written in the **present tense**.

Example ***Follow*** the gravel road until you ***reach*** the highway.

Instructions are **always** written as **commands**. Instructions have no subject, only a verb and an object: Verb + Object.

Example Stop (verb) the noise (object).

1 **Rewrite** the following sentences in the present tense as instructions.

a They rode bikes to school.

____

b We never dive-bombed at the pool.

____

c You listened to the instructions carefully.

____

When we write about things that will happen in the future we use the **future tense** of the verbs in our sentences.

Example It ***will rain*** tomorrow.

2 These sentences are written in the past tense. **Rewrite** them in the **future tense** by changing the verb.

a Lucy walked to school.

____

b The thunderstorm made walking dangerous.

____

c The rules of the game were hard to follow.

____

3 In what tense are these sentences written? **Write** past, present or future beside each one.

a Recipes are directions for cooking food. ____________

b Our coach's instructions helped us win the game. ____________

c The stationmaster will tell us when the next train leaves. ____________

Punctuation—Revision

Add all missing punctuation, including capitals, commas and full stops.
emily ellie esther and eric all belong to the same family, the edwards

Fun with words

1 **Label** each picture with a single word. All the words are in the word box on page 46.

a ____________ **b** ____________ **c** ____________ **d** ____________

2 The red box contains a list of landmarks on the way to Mount Silly Top.

Giggle Pond   Rough and Tumble Slope
Laughing Rock   Greasy Lane   Joke Corner
Jelly Roll Road   Mudbath Hollow
Don't Know Where I Am Crossroads
The Sleepy Tree

a **Draw** a picture of one of these landmarks in the empty box.

b **Write** three instructions to get to the landmark you have just drawn. (You don't have to include all the landmarks in your instructions. Your walker has passed half of them already.)

1 ____

2 ____

3 ____

c **Stand up. Follow** these instructions carefully. When you get to the end, **write** down where you are.

1 Take three steps to the right.
2 Turn left and take three more steps.
3 Turn left again and take three more steps.
4 Turn right and take three steps, then turn right and take three more.

5 Turn right and take six steps.
6 Walk straight ahead three steps.

7 Where are you? ______________________

Your turn to write

Tip for top writers

When you write instructions remember to make them simple, clear and chronological (in the right order).

1 Mr Muddle wants to look at the mountains through his binoculars. This is what he does.

1 He takes the binoculars out of the case.
2 He adjusts the focus so he can see clearly.
3 He holds them to his eyes.
4 He takes the covers off the lenses.

Mr Muddle can't see the mountains. All he can see is a smudgy blur. Check what Mr Muddle did, then **write** him **instructions** for adjusting and using his binoculars correctly. Make sure you write the instructions in the correct order. The first is done for you.

1 Take your binoculars out of their case.

2 ____

3 ____

4 ____

2 **Write** your friend a set of **instructions** for getting to your house from school.

____

____

____

____

____

____

3 You are going on holiday. **Write instructions** for your neighbour to feed your cat and your rabbit while you are away. Use your own paper.

Answers on page 72

Chapter 9 Writing an invitation and a thank-you letter

An **invitation** is written in a mixture of short sentences and points. It gives all necessary information and encourages the reader to accept.
A **thank-you letter** is a short letter with an address, a date, a greeting and a signature. It says thank you at its beginning and its end.

STRUCTURE

LANGUAGE

Birthday party invitation

Greeting → Dear Sally,

Invitation → I'll be nine on Saturday.
Please come and help me celebrate at my house. ← *Full sentences*

Necessary information →
Where: 14 Marlowe Crescent, Brushbox
When: 2–5 pm Saturday, 9.10.05
RSVP: 6.10.05
Phone: 4750 3269
← *Phrases in point form*
(RSVP) ← **Means 'Reply by'**

Personal message → I hope you can come,

Signature → Your friend, Peter

Letter of thanks

Writer's address and date →
14 Marlowe Crescent
Brushbox
15 October 2005

Greeting → Dear Grandfather and Grandma,

Introduction and thank you → Thank you for the book about ships. It was a great birthday present. My friend Shane likes ships too so we are reading it together.

***Body of letter** details of party* → My birthday party was fun. **It didn't rain even though the weather man said it would.** We played cricket and ate lots of fairy bread and birthday cake.

Mum made the cake. **It was shaped like a ship with licorice for funnels and Smarties for portholes.** It looked very real. It was almost a pity to eat it, but we did.

(highlighted sentences) ← Usually written in **full sentences** with correct punctuation

***Conclusion** repeats thanks* → Dad says he will drive us all up to see you. Emma and I hope it will be very soon. Thank you again for my book.

Signature → Love from,
Peter

***Everything starts** at left margin*

What did you read?

1. **Complete** this sentence. ____________ is inviting ____________ to his birthday party.
2. Where will the party be held? ____________________________
3. How old will Peter be on Saturday? ______________________
4. **Complete** this sentence. The party will be held between the hours of _____ and _____ o'clock on Saturday.
5. Who is Peter's friend? _____________________
6. Of what were the portholes made? _____________________
7. Who made Peter's cake? _________________________________
8. What did Peter's grandparents give him for his birthday?

   ____

9. **Complete** this sentence. Peter wrote this letter to say ____________________ to his grandparents.

How is it written?

1. **Circle** the **wrong** answer. Peter's invitation contains:
   - a short sentences
   - b points
   - c headings
   - d explanation of party games
2. **Underline** the three most important things in an invitation.
   - a date and time
   - b pictures of balloons and streamers
   - c venue (place)
   - d name of host (birthday person)
   - e special message from host
3. The reason for writing Peter's letter is clear in the first line. **True or false?** _____________
4. Peter's thank-you letter only talks about the book he received. **True or false?** ____________
5. A letter always starts with a GR _ _ TING and ends with a SIG _ _ TURE.

Spelling and meaning

invitation	real	licorice	Saturday
weather	reel	ferry	present
whether	birthday	fairy	celebration

When you are learning to spell sometimes it helps to break the words up into parts (**syllables**).
Examples invitation: in / vi / ta / tion Saturday: Sat / ur / day

1 **Write** down all the words in the word box that have only one syllable.

____

2 Break the following words into syllables. Use a slash (/) to separate them.

a present ______________________________

b birthday ______________________________

c celebration ______________________________

d licorice ______________________________

3 The word box contains some **homophones** (words that sound the same but are spelt differently and mean different things). **Choose** the correct homophone for these.

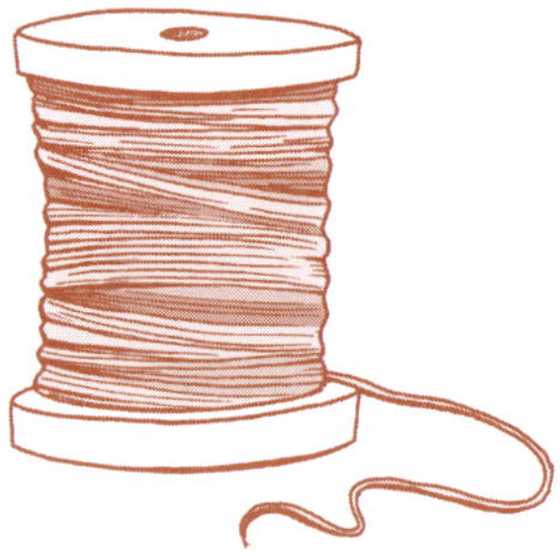

a ______________ b ______________ c ______________

4 **Insert** a word from the word box in the spaces.

a You can cross Sydney Harbour by ______________.

b Stormy ______________ is dangerous for sea travel.

c Eating ______________ can stain your tongue black.

d Kangaroos are ______________ but bunyips and dragons are not.

5 ***Celebrate*** is a **verb**. ***Celebration*** is a **noun**. Following the celebrate/celebration pattern make nouns out of these verbs.

a decorate ______________________ b excavate ______________________

c imitate ______________________ d renovate ______________________

Grammar

Sometimes we write short sentences with only one verb. We call these **simple sentences**.

Example Balloons are fun.

We can join two simple sentences with ***and*** or ***but*** to make a longer sentence called a **compound sentence**.

Example Balloons are fun. Balloons break easily. (two simple sentences)

Balloons are fun ***but*** balloons break easily. (compound sentence)

1 **Join** these simple sentences with ***and*** or ***but*** to make compound sentences.

a Peter invited Ahmad to his party. Ahmad was not able to come.

____

b Your birthday is in summer. My birthday is in winter.

____

c A mouse lives for a year. Some turtles can live for one hundred years.

____

In a compound sentence we can use another word (a **pronoun**) instead of repeating the ***noun***.

Example Balloons are fun but ***they*** break very easily.

(***They*** is a **pronoun**. Other pronouns are ***we***, ***you***, ***he***, ***she***, ***it***.)

2 **Join** these sentences to make compound sentences using ***and*** or ***but*** and a **pronoun**. The first is done for you.

a John went to the newsagent's. John bought twenty red balloons.

John went to the newsagent's and he bought twenty red balloons.

b Katherine cut the cake. Katherine passed a slice to everyone.

____

c Billy liked the birthday cake. Billy liked the toffee apples better.

____

Punctuation

Addresses always start with capital letters, and so do **months** and **days** of the year.

1. Look at the address on Peter's letter and then put **capitals** in the correct places on these addresses.

   a 4 boulder drive rocky point.

   b 312 blackberry road thorny hills

   c 13 lonely lane lost horizon

   d 9 rose place flowerpot

2. **Punctuate** these dates correctly.

   a 24 october, united nations day

   b 25 april, anzac day

Fun with words

1. The fun part of a party is the games we play. Can you play the game of Authors? In this game you have to listen to the sound of the words and then match the authors' names to the names of their books (e.g. Cliff Death by Eileen Dover). Can you hear the meaning in the author's name? **Match** these book titles with their authors' names.

a	George in Gaol	by ______________	Mary Christmas
b	Sleepless Nights	by ______________	Teresa Green
c	On a Desert Island	by ______________	Eliza Wake
d	Colours in Nature	by ______________	E. Dunnit
e	Christmas Time	by ______________	Bob Down
f	Knocked Out	by ______________	I. Malone

2. How many **one-syllable words** can you make out of this word? CELEBRATION

______________ ______________ ______________

______________ ______________ ______________

______________ ______________ ______________

______________ ______________ ______________

3. It is a custom in many countries to associate a precious stone with the month of your birthday (e.g. a person whose birthday is in April has a diamond as his or her birthstone).

   The following are the names of precious stones. Can you **complete** them?

   a PE __ RL

   b R __ BY

   c EM __ R __ LD

   d S __ PPH __ RE

4 If you **answer** these party questions correctly and then put the first letter of each answer together, you will have the answer to the mystery word in question 5.

- **a** What do you do with a birthday present? You __ __ __ N it.
- **b** Girls' presents are usually wrapped in __ __ __ TTY paper.
- **c** We send invitations to __ __ K our friends to our party.
- **d** There are lots of cakes and __ __ LLIES at a party.

5 Mystery word: Precious stone only found in Australia: __ __ __ __

Your turn to write

Tips for top writers

1 When you write an invitation you must include **who**, **when** and **where**.

2 When you write a thank-you letter you must say **thank you**.

1 **Write** and decorate an invitation to your best friend, inviting him or her to come to your birthday party. Use your own paper.

2 **Write** a short letter to your uncle thanking him for taking you fishing. You could have been fishing from a boat, from a river bank or from a wharf.

Address ____________________

____

____

Greeting ____________________

Thank you ____________________

____

What you enjoyed ____________________

____

____

____

____

____

Thank you again ____________________

Signature ____________________

Answers on pages 72–73

Chapter 10 Writing a response to a picture

When we write a **response** to a picture we are writing **facts** (what we see in the picture) and **opinion** (what we think about what is happening in the picture).

When I look at this picture

STRUCTURE

Introduction main idea of picture

I see a traffic jam at an intersection. A car has stopped to let a mother dog cross the road in front of it. Three spotted pups are following her.

Facts and opinion

The driver **waits patiently** while the dogs **trot** across the road. Behind his car other cars **begin** to bank up. Soon lots of cars have stopped.

An old lady coming home from shopping puts her vegetables on the footpath while she watches the pups **anxiously**. A little boy is also watching from the footpath. He seems very worried about the last little pup.

One of the pups, the smallest, is lagging way behind the others. I think his little legs can't run as fast as the others. He looks like the **runt** of the litter.

Reaction what the writer thinks most important about the picture

The man in the first car must be a kind man. Even though the traffic is banked up right around the corner he is not moving. He is not even honking his horn. He is just sitting there waiting for all the dogs to cross the road.

Jack (aged 8)

LANGUAGE

Same tense throughout. This writer uses present tense.

Adverbs tell *how* the waiting and the watching is done

Good choice of noun tells us that this is the smallest and weakest of the pups.

What did you read?

1. **Complete** this sentence. The traffic is banked up right around ______________________.
2. Why did the first driver stop? ____

____
3. The pups are all the same size. **True or false?** ______________
4. How many pedestrians are watching? ______________________
5. What was the old lady doing before she stopped to watch the dogs?

____
6. **Tick** the statement that is correct.
   - a The smallest pup's legs can't run as fast as his brothers' legs.
   - b Jack thinks the smallest pup's legs cannot run as fast as his brothers' legs.
7. Why does the writer think the first driver is kind?

____

____
8. Who is Jack? ______________________________________

How is it written?

1. **Circle** the correct answer. The main idea of the picture is explained in paragraph:
   - a one
   - b two
   - c three
   - d four
   - e five
2. **Complete** the sentence. Jack uses the word P _ _ _ _ _ _ LY to tell us that the driver waited without getting cross.
3. **Circle** the correct answer. Jack tells us:
   - a only what he sees
   - b only what he thinks
   - c what he sees and what he thinks about what he sees
4. Response writing includes **facts** (what the writer sees) and **opinion** (what the writer thinks about what he sees). **Complete** these sentences.

   One **fact** in Jack's writing is ____

   One **opinion** in Jack's writing is ____

Spelling and meaning

intersection	footpath	patient	building
stopped	vegetables	impatient	runt
traffic	anxiously	worried	lagging

Remember to break big words into syllables as you learn to spell them. Take extra care with double letters as in ***worried***. Use the Look, Cover, Write and Check way to learn spelling.

1 **Insert** a word from the word box.

a An ______________ man kept pushing the pedestrian button.

b The sea captain watched the stormy sky ______________.

c There are traffic lights at the ______________ of Todd and Hope Streets.

d Beans, cabbage and broccoli are all green ______________.

2 **Match** the words in **A** to their synonym in **B**.

A		B
a kind		walker
b concerned		little
c small		pavement
d footpath		anxious
e pedestrian		thoughtful

3 The word ***bank*** has many meanings. Read each sentence carefully and then choose from the explanations below the one that best suits the meaning of ***bank*** in that sentence.

a Old Charlie Green fishes from the river ***bank***. ___

b Australia used to have a ***bank*** called the Rural Bank. ___

c In peak hour traffic will ***bank*** up. ___

d I want to ***bank*** my pocket money. ___

Explanations

A **Verb** meaning to save in a bank

B **Noun** meaning a building

C **Noun** meaning the side of a river

D **Verb** meaning to come to a stop in a close line of cars

Grammar

When we **compare** one noun to another we change the form of the adjectives we use.

Example

Mark is ***tall***. Matthew is ***taller***. Luke is ***tallest***.

MARK

MATTHEW

LUKE

1 **Write** the correct form of the adjective in brackets in the spaces.

a Mt Everest is (high) ________________ than Mt Kosciuszko.

b The cheetah is the (fast) ________________ animal on earth.

c Crimson is the (dark) ________________ tone of the colour red.

d Shrubs are (short) ________________ than trees.

Adjectives that end in ***–y*** change the ***y*** to ***i*** before adding ***–er*** or ***–est***.

Example dry → drier → driest

2 ***Change*** these adjectives according to this pattern.

a lovely ________________ ________________

b ugly ________________ ________________

c empty ________________ ________________

d friendly ________________ ________________

e hungry ________________ ________________

Some adjectives have their own special ways of comparing nouns.

Examples good → better → best

far → further → furthest

bad → worse → worst

3 **Write** the correct form of the word in brackets in the spaces.

a John is a good batsman but Songkai is the (good) ________________ bowler.

b Our moon is far away but Jupiter is (far) ________________ away.

c Pluto is the planet at the end of the universe. It is (far) ________________ from Earth.

d All my family had the flu but I had it the (bad) ________________.

Punctuation

Insert all the missing punctuation in this passage.

there are nine planets in our solar system. they are called earth venus mercury mars jupiter saturn uranus neptune and pluto jupiter's beautiful rings are made of gas.

Fun with words

1 Many words mean ***big*** but some are bigger than others. **Write** these ***big*** words in the triangle with the smallest meaning of ***big*** at the top and the largest at the bottom.

big gigantic huge enormous

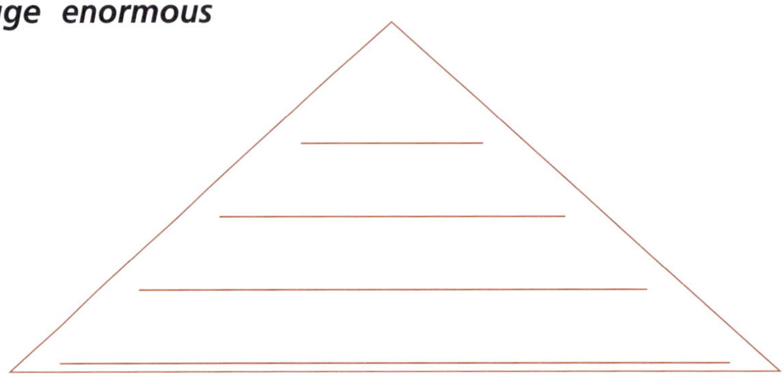

2 These are all ***little*** words. Can you arrange them in order of littleness, ending with the smallest?

small infinitesimal minute tiny

a ____________ **b** ____________ **c** ____________ **d** ____________

3 Can you **guess** the missing word?

a People have ______________, pigs have snouts and elephants have trunks.

b Horses have hooves, people have feet and seals have ______________.

c Fish have scales, koalas have ______________ and people have skin.

d People live in houses, foxes live in dens and bees live in ______________.

4 Most creatures like to live in groups. Here are some group names. Can you **match** them with the creatures they refer to? flock herd pride pod school pack

a a __________ of fish **b** a __________ of lions

c a __________ of wolves **d** a __________ of whales

e a __________ of cattle **f** a __________ of birds

5 When we gather things together we often give them group names too. Can you **complete** these group names?

a a group of ships: F __ __ __ T

b knives, forks and spoons together: C __ TL __ __ Y

c a group of planes: SQU __ D __ __ N

d cups, saucers and plates together: CR __ CK __ __ Y

JOKE

Q. How do you know which end of a worm is its head?

A. Tickle it in the middle and wait till it smiles.

Your turn to write

Tip for top writers

When looking at a picture ask:

- What do I see?
- What do I think?

Choose **one** of these pictures. **Write** a response to the picture according to the plan below. Use your own paper.

Paragraph 1 What is the most important thing happening in the picture?

Paragraph 2 Write some details about the picture.

Paragraph 3 Write some more details about the picture.

Paragraph 4 What do you think when you look at this picture? Would you like to be doing this?

What would you feel like?

Writing for school research projects

When we are asked to gather information on a subject and present it in a book or on a poster we can present the information in two ways:

1 as a **list of facts** in point form written as **phrases**
2 as an **information report** written in **complete sentences**.

STRUCTURE

LANGUAGE

Information report

Koalas

The koala is a small, tree-living marsupial found only in Australia. It used to be called a 'native bear'. The koala's thick woolly fur is grey except on its belly where it is yellowish-white. It has large round, furry ears, small brown eyes and a big flat black nose. Because it lives in trees it has short powerful arms and legs with strong black nails for climbing.

Koalas usually have only one baby at a time and care for it in a pouch under the mother's belly. When the baby is big it hangs onto its mother's belly fur with its claws to be carried when she moves around.

Physical description includes definition in first sentence

Facts about life and habitat

Several related facts in one sentence

Adjectives of shape, size, colour and texture

All verbs in present tense throughout text

Fact boxes

Habits	Dangers
• usually solitary	• timber cutting
• mostly nocturnal	• feral animals
• rarely drinks	• disease called chlamydia
• eats eucalyptus leaves only	• spread of houses
• clumsy on ground	• speeding traffic

Titles tell us what kind of facts are in the boxes

Bullets, numbers, letters etc. highlight facts

All facts presented as short phrases

Sample layouts

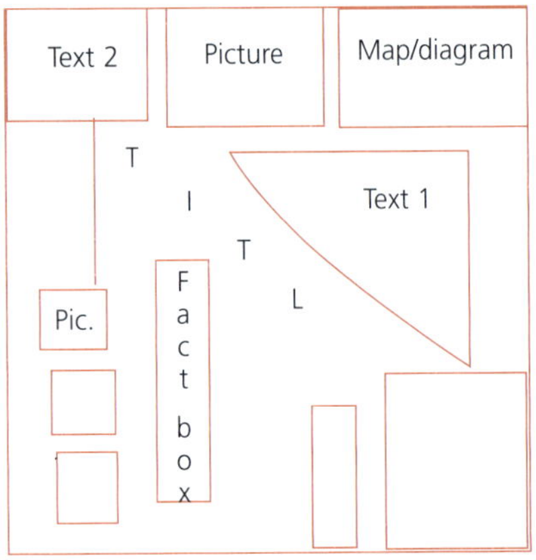

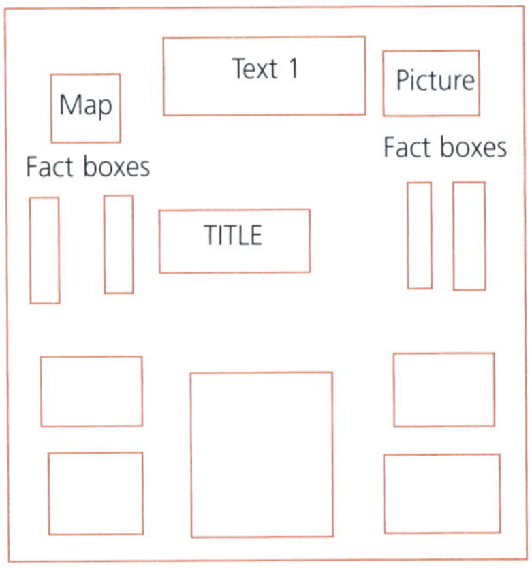

What did you learn?

Complete these sentences about the **information report**.

1. The information report is written in S __ NT __ __ CES.
2. This text D __ SCR __ B __ S what a ________ looks like and why it looks like that.
3. It includes details such as colour and size so we can S __ __ a picture of a koala in our mind.
4. It does N __ T include any opinions, only F __ __ TS.

Complete these sentences about the **fact boxes**.

1. These are written in P __ __ NT form.
2. Points are N __ T complete sentences. They are PH __ __ S __ S.
3. Each point tells us a F __ __ T about the koala or its environment.
4. Points could be listed by N __ __ B __ R, by L __ TT __ R, by symbols like stars or by bullet spots.
5. The facts in each fact box are all related. Facts in Box 1 are all about the K __ __ L __ and those in Box 2 are all about D __ NG __ RS to koalas.

Complete these sentences about the **sample layouts**.

1. There is only one way to arrange a layout. **True or false?** ________
2. Look at both layouts. The following usually occur in all layouts. Can you complete these words?

   a T __ TL __

   b I __ F __ __ M __ TION R __ P __ __ TS

   c P __ CT __ __ __ S

   d F __ __ T BOXES

Your turn to write

1 **Read** the passage and then **write** its most important facts in point form in the **fact box** below.

The waters around Australia are home to more than twenty different kinds of whales. Some of the most interesting are the whalebone whales, which do not have teeth. Instead, they have fringes of whalebone, or baleen, hanging in fine strips from the roof of their mouth. They swim with their mouths open and the baleen strains tiny sea creatures called krill out of the water as their huge tongues push the water out through the baleen.

The largest of the whales is the blue whale. It is the largest mammal that has ever lived, measuring, on average, 27 metres and weighing up to 130 tonnes.

Killer whale

Australian whales

a ____________________

b ____________________

c ____________________

d ____________________

e ____________________

f ____________________

2 **Write** a **fact box** about one of the following: bats whales bushfires policemen stars aeroplanes dolphins seals parrots farms the Great Barrier Reef volcanoes earthquakes

Title:

a ______________________________

b ______________________________

c ______________________________

d ______________________________

e ______________________________

f ______________________________

3 **Read** the facts in the fact box below. Then **rewrite** them as an **information report**. Don't forget to write in complete sentences.

The sperm whale

- 20 metres long
- Huge square head
- Peg-shaped teeth
- Several rows of teeth
- Once killed for its oil
- Now protected

Answers on pages 74–75

Answers

Chapter 1 Pages 2–7

What did you read?

1 Kevin's father
2 on the farm where Kevin lived
3 in Bungendore
4 False
5 False
6 a, c
7 was not
8 to hold the house securely on the trucks

How is it written?

1 True
2 b
3 interesting
4 anything that interested you (e.g. moving the house in two halves)
5 b
6 a

Spelling and meaning

1 a halves
b elves
c calf
d shelves

2 a calf
b halves
c shelves
d elf

3 a half
b shelves
c elves
d calves
e halves

Grammar

1 a Edmund Hillary climbed Mount Everest.
b Snakes eat small birds.
c Storm clouds fill the sky.
d Mr Patel drives a removal truck.

2 a no
b yes
c yes
d no

3 a Five children played marbles.
b All our class plays soccer.
c Mrs Mercado packed her good china.
d A removal truck moved our furniture.
e The gardener planted peas and beans.

Punctuation

1 a full stop
  b question mark
  c full stop
2 **I**n the bush there are no traffic jams to worry drivers. **I**nstead drivers have to worry about dust. **W**hy is this so**? B**ig trucks leave great clouds of dust in the air and this makes it hard for drivers behind them to see where they are going**.**

Fun with words

1 a cow
  b shelves
  c elves
  d half
2 a thistle
  b kangaroo, joey
3 a furniture
  b boxes
  c truck
  d pack
  e removal
  f wrap

Your turn

1 e, b, c, d, a, f

Chapter 2 Pages 8–13

What did you read?

1 a bottle with a message inside
2 c
3 The dolphin swallowed them.
4 a starfish
5 The dolphin took them there.
6 fifteen years
7 a Triton fed them but not very well.
  b They only ate seaweed and plankton.
8 c

How is it written?

1 b
2 a
3 trailed
4 Landcrabs, important, does not
5 'King Triton wants to see you' **or** 'The king is about to make an announcement' **or** 'You will build me a house for every creature in my world, even the smallest of them'

Spelling and meaning

2 a very tiny sea creatures
  b sharp snapping sound
  c any living animal or person
  d sea between continents
3 a tough, enough
  b fruit, bruise

Grammar

1 cupboard, sadness, horse, Australia, paddock, church, shop, ship, George
2 a holidays, sun, sand, surf
  b flags, beach
  c seashells, homes, molluscs
  d starfish, points, arms
  e tide, moon
3 wave, dolphin, ball, fin, beak, eyes, tail, flippers, ocean

Punctuation

When winter is past everyone is happy**. P**eople wear sandals and sun hats**. C**hildren go swimming**. A**dults begin to garden again**. S**mall plants grow tall and seeds turn into plants**. E**ven birds are happy and busy building nests.

Fun with words

1 a octopus
  b shark's and a seal's
  c calf
  d seahorse
  e swordfish
  f starfish
2 a box
  b engine
  c angry

d cub
e hollow
f beach

3 a coral
b blue whale

Chapter 3 Pages 14–19

What did you read?

1 c
2 False
3 We know it is not afraid of people because it sits on Kevin's shoulder.
4 b
5 round
6 False
7 no
8 a

How is it written?

1 Brat rat,/pet rat,/my rat/in my hand.
2 black and white/beady eyes bright
3 shells
4 pink snake tail
5 a
6 a, b, e

Spelling and meaning

1 a beach
b sight
c paint
d light
e dainty

2 a paint
b beach
c saint

3 a teach
b reach
c lead

4 a sight, light, tight
b same

Grammar

1 a sleek, smooth, brown, black
b long, bare, strong, tiny, useless
c old, shabby, crooked
d sweet-smelling, comfortable, pet
e empty, sad, lost

2 a new, clumsy
b happy tropical, glass
c same, lonely
d rough, bad-tempered
e green, gentle

3 a leafy
b sandy
c dirty
d angry
e hungry
f friendly

Punctuation

1 a Seal pups are fat**,** round**,** roly-poly balls of soft fur.
b Magpies build big**,** strong nests high up off the ground.
c Crimson rosellas flash scarlet**,** blue and green in flight.
d Keeping pets is an interesting**,** enjoyable and responsible hobby.

Fun with words

1 Scales: snake, goldfish, python
Fur: rat, mouse, guinea pig, wombat, dog, cat, penguin, dingo
Feathers: eagle, magpie, canary, budgerigar
Skin: frog, lizard, whale

2 a stye
b stable
c burrow
d den
e colony

3 a zoologist
b apiarist
c stockman
d veterinarian

4 a fur
b feathers

c burrow
d bill
e ocean
f hooves

Chapter 4 Pages 20–25

What did you read?

1 b
2 a caterpillar
3 leaves
4 It builds a cocoon.
5 a
6 dry
7 to collect pollen

How is it written?

1 Butterflies are born caterpillars. All caterpillars become moths or butterflies.
2 a hatch
  b pollen
3 b
4 c

Spelling and meaning

1 a pollen
  b leaves
  c cocoon
  d hatch
2 a unlike
  b gather
  c period
  d lovely
3 a caterpillars
  b cocoons
4 spies, flies, skies
5 hooves, calves, elves
6 schools, shelves, houses, horses, babies, dinghies

Grammar

1 a grow
  b hatch
  c is
  d are, travel
  e hatch, scramble, dive, swim
2 a Blue-ringed octopuses live in rockpools.
  b Funnel-web spiders trap insects in sticky webs around their hole.
  c The magpie begins life as an egg, hatches into a fledgling and then grows into an adult bird.
3 are, raise, was, is. The pouch was warm and soft.

Punctuation

Lions**,** tigers**,** jaguars**,** cheetahs and the common house cat all belong to the same family**,** the feline family. Wolves**,** dingoes and jackals are all relatives of our pet dogs.

Fun with words

2 a won't work
  b isn't sensible
  c hasn't eaten
  d is not to be trusted
  e is very strong
  f thinks he/she is special
4 a net
  b book
  c alarm clock

Chapter 5 Pages 26–31

What did you read?

1 b
2 False
3 rice straw
4 c
5 True
6 palm
7 a Mr Lee is not a rich man.
  b His clothes and work tell us he is poor.

How is it written?

1 quiet
2 a wade
  b cast

3 faded blue, ragged, old rice-straw
4 a
5 sunset
6 **a** clothing
b hands
c day's work
d mood
7 past

Spelling and meaning

1 **a** cat, crumbs, lamb
b cat
2 **a** rarely
b quiet
c strengthen
d gracefully
3 **a** hop
b slope
c mop
4 mopped, hopped, sipped, topped, sopped, ripped, tapped, sapped, tipped

Grammar

1 **a** mopped
b sopped
c topped
d mapped
2 **a** The Titanic sank when it **collided** with an iceberg in 1912.
b Pemulwuy **was** a brave Aboriginal warrior who lived around Sydney Harbour in the late 1700s.
c When night **fell** bats came out of their cave.

Punctuation

1 **I**n Australia many people enjoy fishing**.** **O**ne of the most dangerous ways to fish is to fish from rocks at the bottom of a cliff. **B**ig waves often sweep rockfishers into the sea where many drown.
2 **a** Yabbies**,** prawns**,** lobsters**,** crabs
b holey**,** old, red**,** green
c The Lachlan**,** Murray**,** Murrumbidgee and
d feed it**,** train it**,** walk it**,** brush it and

Fun with words

1 **Counting**: needles, rakes, cans, letters, ice-blocks, pumpkins, trees, apples, gates, trucks; **Weighing**: sugar, wheat, powder, ice-cream, custard, rice, gravy, jelly, pepper, soup, jam

Chapter 6 Pages 32–37

What did you read?

1 The most important reason for learning to swim is to prevent people drowning.
2 It strengthens muscles. **or** It puts fresh air in the lungs.
3 a
4 b
5 muscles, fresh air
6 build sand castles, collect shells, dig pools and rivers
7 c

How is it written?

1 All children must learn how to swim.
2 I think it's a very good idea for everyone to learn to swim, don't you?
3 a
4 c
5 b

Spelling and meaning

1 down, dredge, drown, edge, frown, hedge, ledge, town
2 **a** ledge
b hedge
c frown
d straight
e likely
3 **a** pledge
b sow
c row
d towel
e shower

- f growl

4 a probable
  b a close row of shrubs
  c without curves
  d river-cleaning barge
  e large village

Grammar

1 Cathy Freeman, Australia's, Olympic Games, Cathy, Olympics, Sydney

2 a **Common:** sportspeople, runner, player, player; **Proper:** Cathy Freeman, Gavin, Wanganeen, Rugby League, Mal Meninga
  b **Common:** pastimes, swimming, months, end, pools; **Proper:** December, February
  c **Common:** months, year, months, season, summer, winter; **Proper:** December, February, June, August

Punctuation

Waltzing **M**atilda is **A**ustralia's most famous song. **I**t was written by **A**ndrew **B**arton **P**aterson more than a century ago. **A**t the time **P**aterson was visiting **D**agworth **S**tation near **W**inton in **Q**ueensland. **W**altzing **M**atilda was sung in public for the first time on 6 **A**pril 1895**.**

Fun with words

1 a down
  b drown
  c straight

2 a group of grown-ups
  b children in your class
  c member of parliament

3 b aquarium

4 seaweed

Chapter 7 Pages 38–43

What did you read?

1 It is held once a year.

2 It will begin on Monday, 16 June.

3 The sale will end when all the goods are sold.

4 $12.99

5 False

6 a

7 b

How is it written?

1 c

2 exclamation marks

3 b

4 a

5 fantastic, red-hot

Spelling and meaning

1 a brick
  b stick
  c horrific
  d elastic
  e sick

2 a annual
  b believe
  c imagine
  d remote

3 a an apple, a banana
  b An orangutan, a red-haired member
  c an edge

4 Id al Fitr, like Christmas, is **an** annual celebration. Muslims celebrate it with **a** feast just as Christians celebrate Christmas with **a** feast.

Grammar

1 a S
  b P
  c P
  d P
  e S

2 a tomorrow
  b overhead
  c wearily
  d today
  e gently

3 a here
  b tomorrow
  c everywhere
  d overhead
  e after

Punctuation

1 Bang!
2 Screech!
3 Help! Help!
4 Penny and Nijmeh read the warning. Danger! No swimming!

Fun with words

3 a False
  b True
  c True

Chapter 8 Pages 44–49

What did you read?

1 c
2 False
3 c
4 He turns left.
5 They must cross in single file because it is narrow and dangerous.

How is it written?

1 b
2 a
3 b
4 a
5 c, d

Spelling and meaning

1 a pacing
  b lacing
  c dicing
  d icing
  e tracing
2 a narrow
  b dangerous
  c Welcome
  d Follow
3 a making right
  b north, south, east, west
  c not wide
  d telling how
4 a safe
  b lead
  c wide
  d unwelcome
5 single file

Grammar

1 a **Ride** bikes to school.
  b Never **dive-bomb** at the pool.
  c **Listen** to the instructions carefully.
2 a Lucy will walk to school.
  b The thunderstorm will make walking dangerous.
  c The rules of the game will be hard to follow.
3 a present
  b past
  c future

Punctuation

Emily**,** **E**llie**,** **E**sther and **E**ric all belong to the same family**,** the **E**dwards**.**

Fun with words

1 a follow
  b narrow
  c correction
  d dangerous
2 c You should be standing exactly where you started.

Chapter 9 Pages 50–55

What did you read?

1 **Peter** is inviting **Sally** to his birthday party.
2 at Peter's house in 14 Marlowe Crescent, Brushbox
3 nine years old

4 The party will be held between the hours of **two** and **five** o'clock.
5 Shane
6 Smarties
7 his mother
8 a book about ships
9 thank you

How is it written?

1 d
2 a, c, d
3 True
4 False
5 greeting, signature

Spelling and meaning

1 reel, real
2 a pres / ent
 b birth / day
 c ce / le / bra / tion
 d lic / or / ice
3 a fairy
 b reel
 c weather
4 a ferry
 b weather
 c licorice
 d real
5 a decoration
 b excavation
 c imitation
 d renovation

Grammar

1 a Peter invited Ahmad to his party but Ahmad was not able to come.
 b Your birthday is in summer and my birthday is in winter.
 c A mouse lives for a year but some turtles can live for one hundred years.
2 a John went to the newsagents and he bought twenty red balloons.
 b Katherine cut the cake and she passed a slice to everyone.
 c Billy liked the birthday cake but he liked the toffee apples better.

Punctuation

1 a 4 Boulder Drive
 Rocky Point
 b 312 Blackberry Road
 Thorny Hills
 c 13 Lonely Lane
 Lost Horizons
 d 9 Rose Place
 Flowerpot
2 a 24 October, United Nations Day
 b 25 April, Anzac Day

Fun with words

1 a E. Dunnit
 b Eliza Wake
 c I. Malone
 d Teresa Green
 e Mary Christmas
 f Bob Down
2 ate, bale, bane, bar, beat, beer, belt, bit, bite, bone, born, brat, cone, core, eat, in, lane, late, lean, lee, leer, lent, lit, nail, near, neat, note, on, rail, rant, rat, rate, real, rear, rent, rib, role, rote, rub, tail, tale, tar, tea, tear, tone (and you may be able to find some more)
3 a pearl
 b ruby
 c emerald
 d sapphire
4 a open
 b pretty
 c ask
 d lollies
5 opal

Chapter 10 — Pages 56–61

What did you read?

1 the corner
2 The first driver stopped to allow the dog and her pups to cross the road.

3 False
4 Two
5 She was shopping for vegetables.
6 b
7 The first driver is kind because he stopped and he is not honking his horn.
8 Jack wrote the response to the picture.

How is it written?

1 a
2 patiently
3 c
4 a There are many facts you could use e.g. traffic jam, dog has three pups, lady puts shopping on the footpath etc.
  b The driver of the first car is a kind man.

Spelling and meaning

1 a impatient
  b anxiously
  c intersection
  d vegetables
2 a thoughtful
  b anxious
  c little
  d pavement
  e walker
3 a C
  b B
  c D
  d A

Grammar

1 a higher
  b fastest
  c darkest
  d shorter
2 a lovelier, loveliest
  b uglier, ugliest
  c emptier, emptiest
  d friendlier, friendliest
  e hungrier, hungriest
3 a better
  b farther
  c farthest
  d worst

Punctuation

There are nine planets in our solar system. **T**hey are called **E**arth, **V**enus, **M**ercury, **M**ars, **J**upiter, **S**aturn, **U**ranus, **N**eptune and **P**luto. **J**upiter's beautiful rings are made of gas.

Fun with words

1

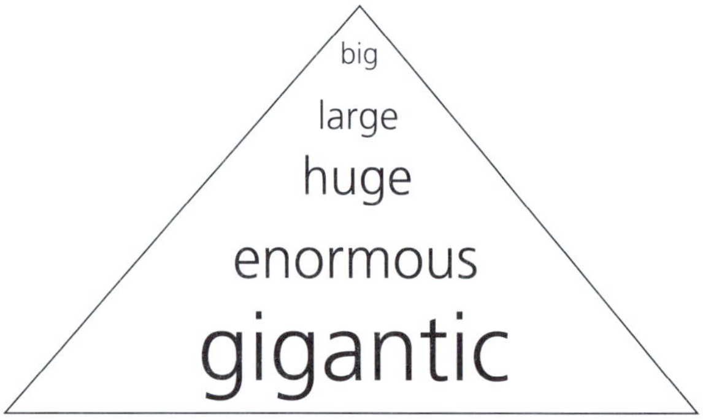

2 a small b tiny c minute
  d infinitesimal
3 a noses
  b flippers
  c fur
  d hives
4 a school
  b pride
  c pack
  d pod
  e herd
  f flock
5 a fleet
  b cutlery
  c squadron
  d crockery

Chapter 11 Pages 62–65

What did you learn?

Information report:

1 sentences

2 describes, koala
3 see
4 not, facts

Fact boxes:

1 point
2 not, phrases
3 fact
4 number, letter
5 koala, dangers

Sample layouts:

1 False
2 a Title
  b Information reports
  c Pictures
  d Fact boxes

Your turn

1 a largest mammal on earth
  b belongs to toothless whalebone family
  c has baleen instead of teeth
  d baleen used to sieve food from water
  e main food, krill
  f average size 27 metres, 130 tonnes

Notes